John Seed

Also by John Seed:

Spaces In (Pig Press, Newcastle-upon-Tyne 1977)
History Labour Night. Fire & Sleet & Candlelight (Pig Press, Durham 1984)
Transit Depots (Ship of Fools, London 1993)
Interior in the Open Air (Reality Street, London 1993)
Divided into One (Poetical Histories, Cambridge 2003)
New & Collected Poems (Shearsman, Exeter 2005)

John Seed

Pictures From Mayhew

London 1850

First published in in the United Kingdom in 2005 by
Shearsman Books Ltd
58 Velwell Road
Exeter EX4 4LD

www.shearsman.com

ISBN 0-907562-62-0

Cover and title-page design by poppodomedia.com

Some parts of this book have previously appeared, or will appear, in *Angel
Exhaust, CCCP Review, Great Works, Pages, P N Review* and *Shearsman*.

The illustrations in this volume are all drawn from Henry Mayhew's
London Labour and the London Poor.

For the student of history.

The publisher gratefully acknowledges financial assistance from
Arts Council England with its 2005-2007 publishing programme.

NOTE: Every word in the pages that follow is drawn from Henry Mayhew's writings on London published in the *Morning Chronicle* from 1849 to 1850, then in 63 editions of his own weekly paper, *London Labour and the London Poor* between December 1850 and February 1852 and then in the four volume work of the same title. The visual images are taken from the latter. An afterword provides further information.

JS

A cab-driver

PREFACE I

If you was to go to
the raffle tonight sir they'd say
directly you come in who's this
here swell what's he want they'd
think you were a cad or
spy come from the police but
they'd treat you civilly some would
fancy you was a fast kind
of a gentleman come there for
a lark but you need have
no fear though the pint pots
does fly about sometimes

PREFACE II

I know who you are well enough

take you for?   why
for a bloody
spy you

here from the Secretary of
State you know you do

to see
how many men I've got in the
house & what kind they are by

God if you ain't soon mizzled I'll
crack your bloody skull open for you

Coal-heavers

I

1

It's no use asking for it
if you wish to keep it
unless you can
lift a horse up
when he's down

2

it's the devil's place of
all you ever saw in your life
standing there before them retorts
with a long heavy rake
pullin out the red-hot coke for the bare life
the rake red-hot in your hands
& the hissin & the bubblin of the water
& the smoke & the smell
it's fit to melt a man like a
roll of fresh butter

3

as we go up the ladder we
very often scrunch our teeth the work's
so hard the coal keeps us from
biting the tongue that's one use the
other is by rolling it along in
the mouth it excites the spittle moistens
the mouth all I want when I'm
at work is a bit of coal

4

We carry the coals in sacks
of 2 cwt.the sack usually weighs
from 14 lb. to 20 lb. so our load
is mostly 238 lb. we carry up
a ladder from the hold of
the ship 16 to 20 feet
deep over four barges over planks
to the waggon 60 to 80
feet with the sacks on our
backs each man will ascend this
height & travel this distance 90
times in a day he will
lift himself with 2 cwt. of coals
on his back 1,460 feet or
upwards a quarter of a mile
high three times the height of
St. Paul's in 12 hours &
besides will travel 6,300 feet or
1¼ mile carrying the same weight
as he goes the labour is
very hard even the strongest cannot
continue for three days together

5

a black nigger slave
was never slaved as I was
I've worked all night
when it's been very moonlight
loading a barge

& I've worked until three
& four in the morning
& then me & another man
slept an hour or two in a
shed as joined his stables
& then must go at it again
I hadn't a rag left to my back
everything was worn to bits
in such hard work
& then I got the sack

6
When I goes
home I just
smokes a pipe
& goes to
bed that's all

II

I sell chickeed & grunsell &
turfs for larks a few nettles
that's ordered they're for tea I
gets chickweed at Chalk Farm out
of the public fields every morning
about seven I goes for it
the grunsell a gentleman gives leave
to get out of his garden
down Battle-bridge way in the
Chalk-road leading to Holloway I
gets there every morning about nine
I gets the nettles at Highgate
after I've gathered my things enough
of each to make up a
dozen halfpenny bunches I puts them
in my basket slings 'em at
my back & starts round London
Low Marrabun I goes to always
of a Saturday & Wednesday I
goes to St. Pancras on a
Tuesday I visit Clerkenwell & Russell
Square & round about there on
a Monday I goes down about
Covent Garden & the Strand on
a Thursday I does High Marrabun
on a Friday I say chickweed
& grunsell as I goes along
I don't say for young singing

birds I'm out in usual till
about five in the evening I
never stop to eat I'm walking
all the time 15 miles every
day of my life I has
my breakfast afoore I starts &
my tea when I comes home

III

I

Mother's been dead a long time
Father gets drunk
sometimes but I think
not so oft as he did

& then he lies in bed
gets up & gets more drink
& goes to bed again

two or three days
& nights at a time

he never uses me badly
when he's drinking
& has money he gives me some

now & then
to get bread & butter with
or a halfpenny pudding
he never eats anything

in the house
when he's drinking
he's a very quiet man

2

when I've been at the worst
I've been really glad I hadn't no one
depending on me

I've smoked a pipe
when I was troubled in mind
& couldn't get a meal

but if I'd had a young daughter now
what good would it have been
my smoking a pipe to comfort her?

when there's others
as you must love
what must it be then?

3

a scurf what he earned
I never knew he gave
me what he liked sometimes
nothing in May last he
gave me 2s. 8d. for the
whole month & two children
they trembled when they heard
his step I can't tell how
we lived then some days
that May we had neither
bite nor sup the water
was too bad to drink
cold they were afraid of

their lives he knocked them
about so drink made him
a savage took the father
out of him his children
was starving but I durstn't
say that aloud when
his mates was by

4
Then I was always thirsty
& when I got up
of a morning I used
to go stalking round
to the first public-house
was open my mouth was
dry parched as if burning
a fever I was ashamed to
be seen out clothes ragged
shoes take the water in
one end let it out the
other I keep my old
rags at home to remind
me I call them the
regimentals of the guzzler

5
Bad as I'm off now
if I had only
a careful partner I
wouldn't want for anything

6

A friend gave me half
a sovereign to bury my
child the parish provided me
a coffin it cost me
about 3s. besides we didn't
have her taken away from
here not as a parish
funeral exactly I agreed that
if he would fetch it
& let it stand in
an open place near his
shop until the Saturday which
was the time I would
give the undertaker 3s. to
let a man come with
a pall to throw over
the coffin so it should
not be seen it was
a parish funeral I had
to give 1s. 6d. for a
pair of shoes before I
could follow my child to
the grave & we paid
1s. 9d. for rent all out
of the half sovereign

IV

1

At Woolwich we were all on the fuddle
at the Dust Hole I went to beg
of a Major whose brother was in Spain
he'd himself been out I said I
was a sergeant in the 3rd Westminster Grenadiers
you know & served under your brother oh
yes that's my brother's regiment says he where
was you then on the 16th of October
why sir I was at the taking of
the city of Irun says I in fact
I was with the costermongers in St. Giles's
calling cabbages white heart cabbages oh then said
he what day was Ernani taken on why
said I a little tipsy & bothered at
the question that was the 16th of October
too very well my man says he tapping
his boots with a riding whip I'll see
what I can do for you the words
were no sooner out of his mouth when
he stepped up to me & gave me
a regular pasting he horsewhipped me up &
down stairs along the passages my flesh was
like sassages I managed at last to open
the door & get away

2

I became a turnpike sailor & went out
as one of the Shallow Brigade wearing Guernsey
shirt & drawers or tattered trowsers there was
a school of four we only got a
tidy living 16s or £1 a day among
us we used to call every one that
came along coalheavers & all sea-fighting captains
now my noble sea-fighting captain we used
to say fire an odd shot from your
larboard locker to us Nelson's bull-dogs but
mind we never tried that dodge on at
Greenwich for fear of the old geese the
Shallow got so grannied in London the supplies
got queer shipwrecks got so common in the
streets I quitted the land navy

3

In wet weather I used to dress tidy
& very clean for the respectable broken-down
tradesman or reduced gentleman caper I wore a
suit of black generally & a clean dickey
& sometimes old black kid gloves & I
used to stand with a paper before my
face as if ashamed:

TO A HUMANE PUBLIC
I HAVE SEEN BETTER DAYS

This is called standing pad with a fakement
it's a wet-weather dodge & isn't

so good as screeving but I did middling
& can't bear being idle

4
I've done the shivering dodge too gone out
in the cold weather half naked one man
can't get off shivering now Shaking Jemmy went
on with his shivering so long he couldn't
help it at last he shivered like a jelly
like a calf's foot with the ague on
the hottest day in summer it's a good
dodge in tidy inclement seasons it's not so
good a lurk by two bob a day
as it once was it's a single-handed job
if one man shivers less than another he
shows it isn't so cold as the good
shiverer makes it out then it's no go

V

I've stood
up to the ankles in snow
till after midnight &
till I've wished I was
snow myself & could melt &
have an end

VI

I

I go of errands some times
fetch water now & then
& post letters but
I do no odd jobs
such as helping the servants to
clean the knives or such-like no
they wouldn't let me behind the
shadow of their doors

2

People going to their offices
six or seven in the morning
gives me a ha'penny or a penny
if they don't I must go without it
I go at five & stand there till
I find it's no use
being there any longer

Oh the gentlemen give me the most
I'm sure the ladies
don't give me nothing never
get anything from servants they
don't get more than they
know what to do with

3

was nigh killed when Queen Caroline
passed through Cavendish-square

after her trial they took the horses
out of her carriage & pulled her along
she kept a chucking money out of the carriage
& I went & scrambled for it
& I got five & twenty shillin
but my hand was a nigh smashed through it
& says a friend of mine before I went
Billy says he don't you go
& I was sorry after I did

4
there was a man
here before me was
obligated to leave &
go into the workhouse
he lost the sight
of one of his
eyes when he came
back again I knew
him sweepin' here a
long time I said
father says I
I went on your crossin'
ah says he you've
got a bad crossin'
poor woman I wouldn't
go on it again
I wouldn't & I
never seen him since

5

Me & Jemmy sold the two of our brooms
for a shilling to two drunken gentlemens

& they began kicking up a row
& going before other gentlemens

& pretending to sweep
& taking off their hats begging

like a mocking of us they
danced about with the brooms

flourishing 'em in the air
& knocking off people's hats

& at last they got into a cab
& chucked the brooms away

VII

I used to carry his tea from his old 'oman
to a old cove as had a stunnin
pitch of fruit in the City-road

but my best friend was Stumpy
had a beautiful crossin
but he's dead now & buried as well

I used to talk to him
& whistle I *can* just whistle
& to dance him the double-shuffle

& he said I
interested him
well he meant he liked it I s'pose

when he went to rest hisself
he soon got tired
over his drop of beer to his grub

I had his crossin'
& his broom for nuff'n
one boy used to say to

Stumpy I'll give you a penny
for your crossin while you's grubbin.
but I had it for nuff'n

& had all I yarned
sometimes a penny sometimes tuppence
only once threepence ha'penny

VIII

1

Bless your heart the smells nothink
it's a roughish smell at first
but nothing near so bad as you thinks
'cause you see
there's such lots o' water always
coming down the sewer
& the air gits in from the gratings
& that helps to
sweeten it a bit

2

when I'd got near the grating in the street
I'd search about in the bottom of the sewer I'd
put down my arm to my shoulder in the mud
& bring up shillings & half-crowns
& lots of coppers
& plenty other things
a silver jug as big as a quart pot
spoons & knives & forks
& every thing you can think of

3

We used to go up the city sewer
at Blackfriars-bridge but
that's stopped up now it's
boarded across inside

'cause of the danger they say
but they don't care
if we haven't got nothing to eat
nor a place to put our heads in

while there's plenty of money
lying there & good for nobody

4

I know a place now
where there's more than
two or three hundredweight of
metal all rusted together
& plenty of money among it too but
it's too heavy to carry it out so it'll
stop there I s'pose
till the world comes to an end

5

I've found sovereigns & half sovereigns
over & over agin
& three on us has often cleared
a couple of pound apiece in one day
out of the sewers but we
no sooner got the money
than the publican had it
I only wish I'd back
all the money I've
guv to the publican
& I wouldn't care
how the wind blew
for the rest of my life

6

You can go a long way in the sewers
if you like I don't know
how far I niver was
at the end on them myself
there's a many branches on ivery side
but we don't go into all we
go where we know
for a cove can't stop in
longer than six or seven hour
cause of the tide you must be out
before that's up

7

If I had my will
I wouldn't allow sewer ratting
for the rats in the shores
eats up a great quantity of
sewer filth & rubbish
& is another specie of scavenger
in their own way

8

The evacuations of the human body
is not only wasted into the Thames but the tide
washes it back again

the water we use is

we drink a solution of our own
faeces
        dead dogs

offal from slaughter-houses
the entrails of animals
pavement dirt stable dung night soil
bodies of murdered men

IX

Wellingtons is cheap
that one's only a halfpenny but
here's one here sir
as you seem to understand coins
as I hope to get 2*d.* for
& will take no less
it's *J. Lackington 1794* you see
& on the back there's a Fame
& round her is written
& it's a good speciment of a coin
Halfpenny of Lackington, Allen & Co.
cheapest booksellers in the world

that's scarcer & more vallyballer
than Wellingtons
or Nelsons either

X

1

Lor bless you them
there stories is the
vonderfullest in the vorld

I'd never ha believed it
if I and't seed it vith my own two hies

but there can't be no mistake
ven I read it hout o' the book

can there now I jist
asks yer that ere plain question

2

I could read a little when I was a child
but I can't now for want of practice

I likes to hear the paper read if I's resting
but old Bill as often wolunteers
has to spell the hard words so
can't tell what the devil he's
reading about

I don't know much good
that ever anybody as I knows
ever got out of books

they're fittest for idle people

XI

I

books on *every* subject on which a book can be written
bibles testaments prayer-books
companions to the altar sermons
Watts' & Wesley's hymns for they're so cheap now
they're not to be sold second-hand at all

I've dealt in tragedies & comedies
old & new cut & uncut
& farces & books of the opera
music books lots of them
scientific & medical works of every possible kind
& histories & travels & lives & memoirs everything
from a needle to an anchor
poetry aye many a hundred weight
Latin & Greek (sometimes)
& French & other foreign languages
pamphlets I've had by the ton
missionary papers of all kinds
parliamentary papers very largely
railway prospectuses with plans to some of them
nice engravings
& the same with other jointstock companies
children's copy-books & cyphering-books
old account-books of every kind
dictionaries of every sort

I've heard of a page round a quarter of cheese though
touching a man's heart

2

I've often cleared out a lawyer's office
bought old briefs & other law papers
& forms that weren't the regular forms then
& any damned thing they had in my line

You'll excuse me sir
I couldn't help thinking
what a lot of misery was caused
by the cwts of waste I've bought at such places

if my father hadn't got mixed up
with law he wouldn't have been ruined
& his children wouldn't have had
such a hard fight of it

I gave three ha'pence a pound
for all I bought at the lawyers
& done pretty well with it but
very likely that's the only
good turn such paper
ever did anyone

unless it were the lawyers

3

An old man dies you see
& his papers are sold off
letters & all
that's the way get rid of
all the old rubbish

as soon as the old boy's
pointing his toes to the sky
what's old letters worth
when the writers are dead & buried?
why perhaps three ha'pennies a pound
& it's a rattling big letter that'll
weigh half-an-ounce

4
Waste-paper I buy
as it comes I
can't read much I
take the backs off
weighs them & gives
a penny & three ha'pence
& tuppence a pound
& there's an end

XII

1

What I shall do in the winter
I don't know

in the cold weather last year
when I could get no flowers
I was forced to live on my clothes

I have none left now
but what I have on

What I shall do I don't know

I can't bear to think on it

2

I looks out every morning
when the costermongers
starts for the markets
& wants boys for their barrers

I hopes to have a barrer of my own
some day & p'raps a horse
I'd go to Epsom then
I don't know how but

3

Poverty's despised among costers
people that's badly off among us

are called cursed
in bad weather it's common
for costers to curse themselves
well I'm cursed they say
when they make no money
it's a common thing to shout
after any one they don't like
that's reduced
well ain't you cursed?

4
in the Lord's prayer
they says forgive us
our trespasses as we
forgives them as
trespasses agin us it's
a very good thing
in coorse but
no costers can't do it

5
The streets *must* be
done as they're done now it
always was so &
will always be so they
must have been like
what they is now yes
there was always streets or
how was people that has tin
to get their coals taken to them

& how was the public-houses to
get their beer?

6

Sold again Chestnuts all hot a penny
a score A halfpenny a skin blacking
Buy buy buy Half-quire o' paper
for a penny A halfpenny a lot
inguns Twopence a pound grapes Three a
penny Yarmouth bloaters Who'll buy a bonnet
for fourpence Pick 'em out cheap here
three pair for a halfpenny bootlaces Now's
your time beautiful whelks a penny a
lot Here's ha'p'orths Come & look at
'em toasters Penny a lot fine russets

*Now here is what we call rough cod he told me they were three days
old he thought it was eatable now he said the eyes were thick and
heavy and sunken and the limp tails of the fish dangled over the
ends of the barrow he said it was a hanging market today things
had been dear and the hucksters couldn't pay the price for them he
said he should fancy the man had probably paid for the fish from
9d. to 1s. each at the rate of 1d. per lb he was calling them at 1½d
he would not take less than this until he had got his own money in
and then probably if he had one or two left he would put up with
1d. per lb the weight he was "working" was 12 oz. to the pound
with the draught of two ounces in the weighing machine and the
ounce gained by placing the fish at the end of the pan would bring
the actual weight given to nine ounces per pound and probably he
had even a lighter pound weight ready for a scaly customer*

7

Why I can assure you
there's my missis she sits
at the corner with fruit
eight years ago she'd have
taken 8s. out of that
street on a Saturday &
last Saturday week she had
one bushel of apples cost
1s. 6d she was out from
ten in the morning till
ten at night & all
she took that day was
1s. 7½d

8

We're all trying to cut
one another down we all
want a livelihood & unless
we did cut one another
down we couldn't get it
if you go down into
Clare-market you'll see that
one butcher is a-striving like
us all to cut his
neighbour's throat by selling cheaper
than him & the shopkeeper
won't let us sell near
him because we can sell
cheaper

9

I know very well
two wrongs can
never make a right but
tricks shopkeepers
practise to grow rich
we must practise to
live at all as
long as they give
short weight & short measure
the streets can't help
doing the same

XIII

Morning twilight the paved court a boy
about five blue naked feet treading the cold
stones a cat over wet ground November
Monday Farringdon vegetable market

I

If we was to go to
Covent-garden to buy 'em we
couldn't do nothing with 'em all
tied up in market bunches but
at Farringdon-market they are sold
loose out of big hampers they
give you a large handful for
a penny the usual time to
go to the market is between
five & six I'm generally down
in the market by five I
was there this morning at five
& bitter cold it was I
give you my word we poor
old people feel it dreadful years
ago I didn't mind cold but
I feel it now cruel bad
to be sure sometimes I'm turning
up my things I don't hardly
know whether I've got 'em in
my hands or not can't even
pick off a dead leaf but
that's nothing to the poor little

things without shoes I've seen 'em
stand & cry two and three
together with the cold my heart
has ached for 'em over &
over again I've said to 'em
I wonder why your mother sends
you out they said they were
obligated to try & get a
penny for a loaf for breakfast

2
some begin crying their
cresses through the streets
at half-past six others
about seven they go
to different parts there
is scarcely a place
but what some goes
to there are so
many of us now
there's twenty to one
to what there used
to be they're so
thick down the market
in summer time you
might bowl balls along
their heads & all
a-fighting for cresses
a regular scramble to
get at 'em to

make a halfpenny at
Farringdon market between four
& five in the
morning & as fast
as they keep going
out others keep
coming in

3
I ain't child
nor woman 'til twenty but
I'm past eight I am

I go about the streets
crying four bunches a
penny water-creases I have to

be down at Farringdon-market
between four & five it's cold before
winter comes on reglar specially

getting up of a morning in the dark
by the light of the lamp in the court when
snow's on the ground it hurts

to take hold of the creases
specially when we takes 'em
to the pump to wash no

I never see any
children crying it's
no use

though the weather was severe she was dressed in a
thin cotton gown a threadbare shawl wrapped round
her shoulders no covering to her head long rusty
hair stood out in all directions when she walked
she shuffled along for fear the large carpet slippers
should slip off her feet

XIV

1

There's a shop round here
makes farthing's worths
of everything a farthing's
worth of sugar a
farthing's worth of
coffee butter & bacca
a halfpenny worth of bread a
farthing's worth of that
ain't no good

2

Aye sir there's more things
every now & then
comes to the stalls
& there used to be still more
when I were young but
I can't call them all to mind
for times is worse with me
& so my memory fails but
there used to be a good many
bayonets & iron tinder-boxes
& steels for striking lights I
can remember
them

3

& if it's a nice thing sir
& perticler if it's a chintz
& to be had for 6d.
the women'll fight for it

4

I should do
much better if
people would only
pay what they
owe but there are
some who never
think of paying
anything

5

Ah! indeed in my time
& before I was married
I have sold different things
in a different way but

I'd rather not talk about that

& I make no complaints
for seeing what I see I'm
not so badly off

XV

1

Ni-ew mackerel
6 a shilling

Ni-ew mackerel
6 a shilling

Ni-ew mackerel
6 a shilling

I've got a good jacketing
many a Sunday morning
for waking people up
crying mackerel
but I've said
I must live while
you sleep

2

We all of us
thanks God for everything
even for a fine day as for
sprats we always says
they're God's blessing for the poor
& thinks it hard of the Lord Mayor
not to let 'em come in
afore the ninth of November
just because he wants to dine off them

which he always do yes we
knows for certain they eats
plenty of sprats
at the Lord Mayor's blanket

3
Ah! Sir sprats
is a blessing to the poor
fresh herrings is a blessing too
& sprats is young herrings
& is a blessing in 'portion

I'm thinking I'll work the country
with a lot they'll keep
to a second day
when they're fresh to start
specially if its frosty weather too
& then they're better than ever yes
& a greater treat
scalding hot from the fire
in the winter time

I hardly know which way
I'll go if I can get
anythink to do among horses
in the country
I'll never come back

4
When a good person
is dying we says

the Lord has called
upon him & he
must go but I
can't think what it
means unless it is
that an angel comes
like when we're a-dreaming
& tells the party
he's wanted in heaven

5
Sparrows are sold in the streets a penny each
sometimes a ha'penny
& sometimes a penny ha'penny
ten thousand every year
as playthings for children
strings are tied to their legs
offering to fly away they are
checked & kept
fluttering in the air
as a child will flutter a kite

XVI

I've seen chess played & I should
say it's a rum game but I
know nothing about it I once had
a old gent for a customer &
he was as nice & quiet a
old gent as could be & I
always called on him when I thought
I had a curus old teacaddy or
knifebox or anything that way he didn't
buy once in twenty calls but he
always gave me something for my trouble
he used to play at chess with
another old gent & if after his
servant had told him I'd come I
waited 'til I could wait no longer
& then knocked at his room door
he swore like a trooper

XVII

1

we generally cry as we go
any old clothes to sell or
exchange & I look down the
area & sometimes knock at the door

2

A good tea service we give
for a left-off suit of
clothes hat & boots they must
all be in a decent condition
to fetch as much as that
we give a sugar-basin for
an old coat & a rummer for
a pair of old Wellington boots
for a glass milk-jug I
should expect a waistcoat & trousers
they must be tidy ones too

3

the china & crockery bought by
hucksters at the warehouses are always
second-rate articles they are most
of them a little damaged &
the glass won't stand hot water

4

but there's nothing so saleable as
a pair of old boots to

us there's always a market for
old boots when there is not
for old clothes you can always
get a dinner out of old
Wellingtons but coats & waistcoats there's
a fashion about them & what
pleases one don't another I can
sell a pair of old boots
going along the streets if I
carry them in my hand the
snobs will run after us to
get those the backs are so
valuable

5
old beaver hats & waistcoats are
worth little or nothing old silk
hats there's a tidy market for
bought for the shops & made
up into new hats for the country
the shape is what is principally
wanted we won't give a farden
for the polka hats with the
low crowns if we can double an
old hat up & put it
in our pockets it's more valuable
than a stiff one we know
the shape must be good to
stand that as soon as a
hatter touches a hat he knows

by the touch or the stiffness
whether it's been through the fire

6

we purchase gentlemen's left-off wearing
apparel mostly sold to us by
women wives of tradesmen or mechanics
mistresses of houses are she-dragons
wants a whole dinner chany service
for their husband's rags as for
plates & dishes they think can
be had for picking up many
a time they sells their husband's
things unbeknown to 'em & often
the gentleman of the house coming
up to the door seeing us making
a deal for his trousers maybe
puts a stop to the whole
transaction often & often I've known
a woman to sell the best
part of her husband's stock of
clothes for chany ornaments for her
mantelpiece & I'm sure the other
day a lady stripped the whole
of her passage & gave me
almost a new great coat hanging
up in the hall for a
few trumpery tea-things

7

but the greatest screws we have
to deal with are ladies in
the squares they stops you on
the sly in the streets &
tells you to call at their
house at sitch a hour of
the day & when you goes
there they smuggles you quietly into
some room by yourselves & sets
to work Jewing away as hard
as they can prizing up their
own things & downcrying yourn why
the other day I was told
to call at a fashionable part
of Pimlico so I gave a
woman 3d to mind the child
& me & my good woman started
off at eight in the morning
with a double load but bless
you when we got there the
lady took us both into a
private room unbeknown to the servants
& wanted me to go &
buy expressly for her a green
& white chamber service all
complete with soap trays & brush
trays together with four breakfast cups
all this here grand set-out
she wanted for a couple of

old washed-out light waistcoats &
a pair of light trousers she
tried hard to make me believe
the buttons alone on the waistcoats
was worth 6d. a piece but
I knowed the value of buttons
afore she were born at first
start-off I'm sure they wouldn't
have cost 1d. each so I
couldn't make a deal of it
no how & I had to
take all my things back
for my trouble

8
if I go out with a
15s. basket of crockery may be
after a tidy day's work I'll
come home with a shilling in
my pocket perhaps I'll have sold
a couple of tumblers or half
a dozen plates & a bundle
of old clothes two or three
old shirts a coat or two
a suit of left-off livery
a woman's gown may be or
a pair of old stays a
couple of pair of Wellingtons a
waistcoat or so these I'd have
at my back & the remainder

of my chany & glass on
my head & werry probably a
humberella or two under my arm
& five or six old hats
in my hand this load altogether
will weigh about three-quarters of
a hundredweight & I shall have
travelled fifteen miles with that at
least for as fast as I
gets rid on the weight of
the crockery I takes up the
weight of the old clothes I
hardly know the value on till
I gets to the Clothes Exchange
in Houndsditch

XVIII

It would take £1 to start me
well I could go to market &
buy my draught of eels a shilling
cheaper & I could afford to cut
my pieces a little bigger & people
where they gets used well comes again
don't you see I could have sold
more eels if I'd had 'em today
& soup too why there's four hours
of about the best time tonight that
I'm losing now cause I've nothing to
sell the man in the market can
give more than we can he gives
what's called the lumping ha'p'orth that is
seven or eight pieces ah that I
dare say he does some of the
boys has told me he gives as
many as eight pieces & then the
more eels you biles up the richer
the liquor is & in our little
tin-pot way it's like biling up
a great jint of meat in a
hocean of water in course we can't
compete agin the man in the market
& so we're being ruined entirely the
boys very often comes & asks me
if I've got a farden's-worth of
heads the woman at Broadway they tells

me sells 'em at four a farden
& a drop of liquor we chucks
'em away there's nothing to eat on
them but the boys will eat anything

XIX

I'm satisfied the 'osses' arts
is sold for beastesses'
'cause you see sir
there's nothing as 'ud be
better liked for favourite cats
& pet dogs than a
nice piece of 'art

but ven do you see the 'osses' 'arts
on a barrow

if they don't go to the cats
vere does they go to

vy
to the Christians

XX

1

Pies all hot meat & fruit
pies all hot I was out
myself last night from four in
the afternoon till half-past twelve
& went from Somers-town down
to the Horse Guards & looked
in at all the public-houses
on the way & I didn't take
above 1s.6d I have been out
sometimes all those hours & haven't
taken more than 4d. & out
of that I have had to
pay a penny for charcoal people
when I go into houses often
begin at me crying Molrow &
Bow-wow at me but there's
nothing of that kind
meat you see is so
cheap now

2

Toss or buy up & win
em if it wasn't for tossing
we shouldn't sell one I've taken
as much as 2s. 6d. at tossing
few people buy without tossing &
the boys in particular gentlemen out

on the spree at the late
public-houses will frequently toss when
they don't want the pies &
when they have won they will
amuse themselves by throwing the pies
at one another or at me
the boys have the greatest love
of gambling & they seldom if
ever buy without tossing sometimes I
have taken as much as
half-a-crown & the people
has never eaten a pie

XXI

1

The generality of persons
we serve take out
their eyes when they
go to bed sleep
with them under their
pillow or in a
tumbler of water on
the toilet-table most
married ladies never take
their eyes out at all

2

Some people wear out
a false eye in
half the time of others
from the increased secretion
of the tears which
act like acid on
metal corrodes & roughens
the surface produces inflammation
& a new eye becomes
necessary the Scotch lose
a great many eyes
& the men in this
country lose more eyes
nearly two to one

3
False eyes are a
great charity to servants
if they lose an
eye no one will
engage them

XXII

1
Hi! hi!

walk inside! walk inside!

& have your c'rect likeness took

frame & glass complete

& only 6*d*.!

time of sitting
only four seconds!

2
It was wonderful
the sight of
children that
had been took

when *one* girl comes for her portrait
there's a dozen
comes along with her to
see it took

3
I lodged in a room in Lambeth
& I used to take them in the back-yard a

kind of garden I used to
take a blanket off the bed
& used to tack it on a clothes-horse
& my mate used to hold it
if the wind was high
whilst I
took the portrait

4
I had one fellow for
a half-guinea portrait &
he was from Woolwich &
I made him come three
times like a lamb &
he stood pipes & bacca
& it was a thundering
bad one after all he
was delighted swears now it's
the best he ever had took
for it don't fade
but will stop black
to the end of the world
though he remarks I deceived
him in one thing for
it don't come out bright

5
Once a sailor came in
was in haste I
shoved on to him the

picture of a carpenter who was
to call in the afternoon
for his portrait the
jacket was dark but
there was a white
waistcoat I persuaded him
was his blue Guernsey
had come up very light
he was so pleased
he gave us 9*d*. instead of 6*d*

people don't know their
own faces half of 'em
never looked in a glass
half a dozen times
directly they see a pair of
eyes & a nose
they fancy their own

6
people prefers more
to be took by a woman than by a man

many's a time a lady
tells us to send that man away
& let the missis come it's
quite natural
for a lady don't mind
taking her bonnet off
& tucking up her hair or

sticking a pin in here & there
before one of her own sect which
before a man proves
objectionable

7
It's a very neat little picture
our sixpenny ones is
with a little brass rim round them
& a neat metal inside
& a front glass so
how can that pay if you
do the legitimate business the glass
will cost you 2d. a-dozen this small size
& you give two with every picture
then the chemicals will cost
quite a halfpenny & varnish
& frame & fittings about 2d. we
reckon 3d. out of each portrait
& then you see there's
house-rent
& a man at the door & boy at the table
& the operator all
to pay out of this 6d.
so you may guess
where the profit is

8
Sunday is the best day
for shilling portraits

people have got their wages &
don't mind spending

Sunday & Monday is the Derby-day like

& then after that they're
about cracked up &
done

9
The only bad money
we have taken was
from a Methodist clergyman who
came in for a 1s. 6d. portrait he
gave us a bad sixpence

XXIII

Hampton Court has the call
for excursions in vans
because of free-trade in the palace
there's nothing
to pay for admission

there's a recommendable & a
respectable behaviour they
generally carry a fiddler with them
sometimes a trumpeter or else
some of them is master of an instrument
as goes down they generally
sings There's a Good Time Coming
& The Brave Old Oak
sometimes a nigger-thing but not so often

they carry their own eatables
& drinkables take them on the grass
very often they walk through the Palace
& sometimes dance on the grass
after that but not for long it
soon tires dancing on the grass

XXIV

I

I imitate all the animals
of the farm-yard on my
fiddle I imitate the bull
the calf the dog the
cock the hen when she's
laid an egg the peacock
& the ass I studied
from nature I never was
in a farmyard in my
life but I went &
listened to the poultry anywhere
in town the Smithfield cattle
gave me the study for
the bull & the calf
my peacock I got at
the Belvidere-gardens in Islington
the ass is common & so
is the dog & them
I studied anywhere though I
had never heard of such
a thing before by constant
practice I made myself perfect

2

When we are out pitching the finest
place is where there is anybody sick
if we can see some straw on
the ground or any tan we stays

we are sure to play up rattle
away at the banjos where the blinds
are down & down will come the
servant saying you're to move on I'll
pretend not to understand we don't move
for less than a bob for sixpence
ain't enough for a man that's ill

3
once I was whistling
before a gentleman's house at
Hounslow he sent his servant
& called me into a
fine large room full of
looking-glasses time-pieces pictures
three fine brass-wire cages
with a bird in each
slung all of a row
from the ceiling he told
me if I'd whistle &
learn his birds to sing
he'd give me a sovereign
I set to work like
a brick & the birds
begun to sing directly &
I amused 'em very much
& let 'em have all
sorts of tunes & he
gave me a sovereign &
I had dinner in the
kitchen with the servants

4

A poor woman in the workhouse
first asked me to learn music she
said it would always be a bit of bread for me I
did as she told me
& I thank her to this day
for it it took me just five months
to learn the cymbal if you
please the hurdygurdy ain't
it's right name the
first tune I ever played was
God save the King the
Queen as is now

5

I've been blind twelve years

we had five children all dead now
& at my husband's death
I was left almost destitute

I used to sell a few laces in the street
but couldn't clear 2s. 6d. a week by it

I had a little help from the parish
but rarely & at last I could get
nothing but an order for the house

a neighbour a tradesman then
taught me to play the violin
but I'm not a great performer
I wish I was

I began to play in the streets five years ago
I get halfpennies in charity
not for my music
some days 2s.
some days only 6d.
& on wet days nothing

my chief places
when I've only the dog to lead me
are Regent street & Portland-place
& really people are very kind
& careful in guiding & directing me
even the cabmen

6
The police are very quiet to us
when anybody throw up a window &
say go on I go sometime they
say there is sick in the house
when there is none but I go
just the same if I did not
then the policeman come & I get into
trouble I have heard of the noise
in the papers about the organs in
the street but we never talk of
it in our quarter they pay no
attention to the subject for they know
if anybody say go then we must
depart that is what we do

XXV

1

Have I got a young man?
missus don' permit no followers
he's in the army
not a officer but a soldier
I goes out along of him
on Sundays leastways
on Sunday afternoons
& missus she lets me go
to see a aunt of mine
as I says lives at Camberwell only
between you & me sir
there ain't no aunt
only a soldier which
he's my sweetheart

2

I listed for a
soldier in the 48th
I liked a soldier's
life very well until
I got flogged 100
lashes for selling my
kit for a spree
& 150 for striking
a corporal who called
me an English robber
he was an Irishman

I was confined five
days in the hospital
after each punishment it
was terrible like a
bunch of razors cutting
at your back your
flesh dragged off to
this day I feel
a pain in my
chest from the triangles

3
I have sold nuts & oranges to soldiers
they never say anything rude to me never

I was once
in a great crowd
& was getting crushed
& there was a very tall soldier
close by me & he lifted me
basket & all right up to his shoulder
& carried me clean out of the crowd

He had stripes on his arm

I shouldn't like you
to be in such a trade says he
if you was my child

XXVI

1

I had eleven children
I'm grandmother to fifteen
a great-grandmother too

they won't give me
a bite of bread
though any of 'em

I've got four children
living as far as
I know two abroad

two home here with
families I never go
among 'em it's not

in my power to assist
'em so I never
go to distress 'em

2

It's only them that's got
a father or mother as
can get a bit of
meat here are many as
ain't got no father nor
mother & they sleeps under

the arches or else in
some of them ere houses
that nobody lives in

3
half-hungered on the road last
winter eating turnips out of this
field carrots out of that sleeping
under hedges & haystacks I slept
under one haystack & pulled out
the hay to cover me &
the snow lay on it a
foot deep in the morning I
slept for all that but wasn't
I froze when I woke it's
hard to hunger for nights together

4
starving about the streets I never
slept in a bed since I've been in London
I generally slept under the dry arches
in West-street where they're building houses
I mean the arches for the cellars

I begged chiefly from the Jews
about Petticoat-lane they all give away
bread their children leave
pieces of crust & such like I would
do anything to be out of this misery

5
if I was to go
into the House I
shouldn't live three days

it's not that I
eat much a very little
is enough for me

but it's the air I
should miss
to be shut up

like a thief
I couldn't live
long I know

Asylum for the Houseless Poor Cripplegate dusk
waiting shivering in the piercing wind cobwebby
garments in tatters the shoeless keep one foot on
the ground bare flesh blue on the snow

XXVII

I

My father was a working silversmith
had the pension from the Goldsmiths'
Company before he died these were
his things I had no brothers
nor sisters & they came to
me after his & mother's death
I've been obliged to part with
some because I was in need
of money & I only see
now the prospect of parting with
them all I can't maintain myself
a great while longer by my
work & then I have nothing
left but to live on them
as long as they will last
& after all to end my
days in the workhouse it's impossible
for me to save a farthing
I can barely live on what
I get I've worked hard all
my life & been unable to
get anything more than would barely
keep me 6d. a day is
all I have had to find
me in coals clothes & food
for these ten years past I
am quite alone in the world

if a place in some almshouse
could be got for me that
would be a real blessing indeed
worth more to me than all
the money in the world

2

I've done for the soldier
from his gaiters to his
cap & I should like
the Queen to see the
state I'm in I wish
she'd come that's all I've
worked for both her uncles
& her grandfather & now
in my old age I'm obliged
to do anything I can
get hold of to get
a crust I find the
work come harder & harder
to me working upon the
red then upon the white
& now tonight acoming to
the black I know it
makes my eyes ache

3

My husband was a file-cutter
did pretty fairly while he was
alive I didn't want for anything

& since his death I've wanted
very often I've wanted so as
I haven't had a home to
put my head into then I
slept along with different friends &
they gave me a little bit
but they were nigh as bad
off as myself & couldn't spare
much there are a many of
us starving yes indeed there is
the old people in particular the
young-uns make it out other ways

4
we're never out from
Monday morning till Saturday night

if I've got nothing to do it's
no use going & making an uproar about

I'm very certain there's no one about here
has got nothing to give me
& I'm very certain opening my mouth won't fill
theirs

& when I've got work why
I sits hard to it
& is glad to have it to do

5

The greatest comfort would be something
more on our beds we lay
dreadful cold of a night on
account of being thin clad I
have no petticoats at all no
blankets of late years warm clothing
would be the greatest blessing I
could ask I'm not at all
discontented at my lot that wouldn't
mend it we strive & do
the best we can & may
as well be contented over it
I think it God's will we
should be as we are providence
is kind to me badly off
as we are I know it's
all for the best

6

You see my hip is
out I used to go
out washing & walking in
my pattens I fell down
my hip is out of
the socket three-quarters of
an inch & the sinews
drawn up I am obliged
to walk with a stick
I couldn't get my living
as I'd been used to

do I couldn't stand a
day if I got five
hundred pounds for it I
must sit down so I
got a little stall &
sat at the end of
the alley here with a
few laces & tapes &
things I've done so for
this nine year past &
seen many a landlord come
in & go out of
the house I sat at
& many a time I've
sat ten & fourteen hours
in the cold & wet
& some days I'd make
a shilling & some days
less

7
I hadn't a
pinch of snuff
for two days
until a friend
gave us a bit
out of his
box it came
very acceptable I
can assure you
it quite revived

me that's all
I'm extravagant in
I can't say
but what I
likes my pinch
of snuff but
even that I
can't get

XXVIII

My husband has been dead
seven year I wish he wasn't
I have no children
alive I worked at the slop trade

while he was alive I was very happy
& comfortable while he lived I was
always true to him
while he was alive so help me God

after his death I was penniless
with two young children.
the only means I had of keeping myself
& the little ones

slop work
brought me in about 5s.6d. a week
two year after his father
I couldn't afford to bury him

my sister paid first-hand
to keep me & my two boys
when my eldest boy died
& for the funeral

I was very thankful to the Almighty
when he took him from me
he died of scarlatina I hadn't
enough to feed him

my second boy's been dead five months
hooping-cough
I loved him as I did my life but I was glad
he was took from me

for I know he's better now
than I could have done for him
the worst kind of poverty
& God only knows what might have become of him

if he had lived my security
died five year ago I was obligated
to go & work for a sweater
a heavy blow

I was getting about 5s. 6d. a week
before then the trowsers was better paid for
& when I was obligated to work second-handed
one of my boys was alive

I couldn't get more than 4s & we could
not live upon the money I
applied to the parish
& they wanted me to go into the house

but I knew they'd take my boy from me
& I'd suffer anything first
at times I was so badly off
it was impossible

to get food & clothing
out of 4s. a week
I was forced to prostitution
to keep us from starving

to get more money
I blush to mention I was
obligated to walk the streets
for money of a night so help me God

XXIX

1

Translation is
to take a worn
old pair of
shoes or boots &
make them appear as if
left off with hardly any wear
as if they were only soiled

2

I should like a few of
them there slop-masters
that's making fortins
out of foolish or greedy
folks to have to
live a few weeks in the streets
by this sort of second-hand trade they'd
hear what was thought of them then
by all sensible people which
aren't so many as they should be
by a precious long sight

3

if you find a slop thing
marked a guinea I don't care
what it is but I'll undertake
you'll get one that'll wear longer
& look better to the very last

second-hand at less than half the money
plenty less it was
good stuff
& good make at first
& hasn't been abused
& that's the reason why it always bangs a slop
because it was good to begin with

4
My customers are nearly all
working people some of them
very poor with large families

for anything I know some of them
works with their heads though
I've noticed their hands is
smallish & seems smoothish
& suits a tight sleeve very well I
don't know what they are
how should I?

XXX

1

I'm called down here the Battersea otter
for I can go out at four
in the morning & come home by
eight with a barrowful of freshwater fish
nobody knows how I do it because
I never takes no nets or lines
I assure them I ketch 'em with
my hands which I do but they
only laughs increderlous like
I knows the fishes' harnts
& watches the tides

2

I've been bitten nearly everywhere & right
through my thumb nail too which as
you see always has a split in
it though it's years since I was
wounded I suffered as much from that
bite as anything it went right up
to my ear I felt the pain
in both places at once a regular
twinge like touching the nerve of a
tooth the thumb went black & I
was told I ought to have it off

I once had the teeth of a
rat break in my finger which was

dreadful bad & swole & putrified so
that I had to have the broken
bits pulled out with tweezers

when the bite is a bad one
it festers & forms a hard core
big as a boiled fish's eye
in the ulcer & hard as
a stone which is very painful &
throbs & after that core comes away
unless you cleans 'em out well the
sores even after they seemed to be
healed break out over & over again
& never cure perfectly

3

I used to wear a costume of
white leather breeches & a green coat
& scarlet waistkit & a gold band
round my hat & a belt across
my shoulder I used to have my
belts painted at first by Mr Bailey
the animal painter with four white rats
but the idea come into my head
that I'd cast the rats in metal
just to make more appearance for the
belt to come out in the world
I took a mould from a dead
rat in plaster I was nights &
days at it & it give me

a deal of bother I could manage
it no how but by my own
ingenuity & persewerance I succeeded & then
I got some of my wife's sarsepans
& by God I casted 'em with
some of my own pewter-pots I
used to make a first-rate appearance
such as was becoming the uniform of
the Queen's rat-ketcher

4
There are four-&-twenty
changes in a linnet's song
it's one of the beautifullest
song-birds we've got it
sings toys as we call
them sounds we distinguish in
the fancy as the tollock
eeke eeke quake le wheet
single eke eke quake wheets
or eek eek quake chowls
eege pipe chowl laugh eege
poy chowls rattle pipe fear
pugh & poy fear is
a sound like fear as
if they was frightened laugh
is a kind of shake
nearly the same as the
rattle this seems like Greek
to you sir but it's

tunes we use in the
fancy I know the sounds
of all the English birds
& what they say I
could tell you about the
nightingale the black cap hedge
warbler garden warbler petty chat
red start a beautiful songbird
the willow wren little warblers
they are linnets any of
them I've got their sounds
in my ear & my mouth

5
The nightingale is a beautiful song-bird they're
plucky birds too & answer to anybody &
taken in April they're plucked enough to sing
as soon as put in a cage persons
fancy that them nightingales as sings at night
is the only ones living but it's wrong
for many on them only sings in the day

XXXI

1

He was the best dog I ever see
& when I parted with him
for a ten-pound note
a man as worked in the New Road
took & made this model he was
a real beauty was that dog
the man as carved that there
didn't have no difficulty in holdin' him still
becos he was very good at that sort o' thing
& when he'd looked at anything
he couldn't be off doin' it

2

In turning the corners of streets
two or three of them together
one will snatch up a dog
& put into his apron
& the others will stop the lady
& say what's the matter
& direct the party who has
lost the dog in a
contrary direction

3

That Punch is as quiet as a lamb
wouldn't hurt nobody
I frequently takes him through the streets

without a lead sartainly
he killed a cat the t'other afternoon but
he couldn't help that
'cause the cat flew at him
though he took it as quietly as
a man would a woman
in a passion & only
went at her just to save his eyes
but you couldn't easy get him off master
when he once got a holt

4
That there
is a dog it was
as good as any in England
though it's so small I've seen her
kill a dozen rats almost as big as herself
though they killed *her* at last
for sewer-rats are dreadful for
giving dogs canker in the mouth &
she wore herself out with continually killing them
though we always rinsed her mouth out well
with peppermint & water
while she were at work
when rats bite they are poisonous
& an ulcer is formed
which we are obleeged to lance that's
what killed her

5

there was one woman a
black used to get out
on the roof of the house
& throw it to the
cats on the tiles she
brought so many stray cats
round about the neighbourhood parties
in the vicinity complained she
would have the meat 16
pennyworth every day always brought
to her before ten in
the morning or else she'd
send to a shop for
it & between ten &
eleven the noise & cries
hundreds of stray cats was
terrible to hear & when
the meat was thrown to
them on the roof the
riot & confusion & fighting
was beyond description

XXXII

1

The poor people who supply me
with rats are what you may
call barn-door labouring poor for
they are the most ignorant people I
ever come near really you would
not believe people could live in
such ignorance talk about Latin &
Greek sir why English is Latin
to them in fact I have
a difficulty to understand them myself

2

when the harvest is got in
they go hunting the hedges &
ditches for rats
once the farmers had to pay
2d. a-head for all rats
caught on their grounds
& they nailed them
up against the wall but now
the rat-ketchers can get 3d. each
by bringing the vermin up to town the farmers
don't pay them anything
to hunt them in their stacks & barns
they no longer get their 2d. in the country
though they get their 3d. in town

3

there is a wonderful deal of difference
in the specie of rats
the bite of sewer
or waterditch rats is
very bad their
coats is poisonous the water
& ditch rat lives on filth
but your barn-rat is a plump fellow
& he lives on the best of everything he's
well off
there's as much difference
between the barn & sewer-rats
as between a brewer's horse & a costermonger's

4

Rats want a deal of watching
& a deal of sorting now you
can't put a sewer & a
barn-rat together it's like
putting a Roosshian & a Turk
under the same roof I can tell
a barn-rat from a ship-rat
or a sewer-rat in a minute
there's six or seven different kinds of rats
& if we don't sort 'em they
tear one another to pieces

5

A rat's bite is very singular
it's a three-cornered one like a leech's

only deeper of course
& it will bleed for
ever such a time my boys
have sometimes had their fingers
go dreadfully bad from rat-bites
all black & putrid like
aye as black as the horse-hair covering to my sofa
people have said to me you
ought to send the lad to the hospital
& have his finger took off but
I've always left it to the lads
& they've said oh
don't mind it father
it'll get all right by & by &
so it has

6
The best thing I
ever found for a rat-bite
was the thick bottoms of
porter casks
put on as a poultice the
only thing you can do is to poultice
these porter bottoms is so powerful
& draws so
they'll take thorns out of horses' hoofs & feet
after steeplechasing

XXXIII

I

Jemmy the Rake
bound to Bristol
bad beds but
no bugs thank God
for all things

2

Razor George & his moll
slept here the day
afore Christmas
just out of stir for
muzzling a peeler

3

Scotch Mary with driz
bound to Dover
& back please God

XXXIV

1

I never be a bit bad with the cold
it never makes me bad
I've been in Canada
with the 93rd in the winter
in the year '43 was a fearful winter indeed
& the men didn't seem to suffer anything
from the cold but were
just as well as in any other climate
or in England they wore the kilt
& the same dress as in
summer some of them wore the
tartan trowsers when they were not
on duty or parade but
the most of them didn't
not one in a dozen for they
looked upon it as like a woman

2

there's nothing so good
for the cold as
cold water the men
used to bathe their knees
& legs in the cold water &
it would make them ache
for the time but
a minute or two afterwards they were
all right & sweating I've

many a time gone into the water
up to my neck
in the coldest days of the year
& then when I came out
& dried myself &
put on my clothes I'd be
sweating afterwards there can't be
a better thing for keeping away
the rheumatism it's a fine thing
for rheumatism & aches to
rub the part with cold frosty water
or snow it
makes it leave him
& knocks the pains out of his limbs

3
now in London
when my hands are
so cold I can't play
on my pipes I
go to a pump &
wash them in the frosty water
& then dry them
& rub them together
& then they're as warm as ever

XXXV

1

This here is the needle that completes our tools
& is used to sew up our cativa stumps
Punch's breeches & Judy's petticoats
& his master's old clothes when they're in holes
I likes to have everything tidy & respectable
not knowing where I'm going to perform to
for every day is a new day that we
never see afore & never shall see again
we do not know the produce of this world
being luxurant (that's moral) being
humane kind & generous to
all our society of life we mends our cativa
& slums when they gets teearey
if you was to show that to
some of our line they'd be
horrified they can't talk so affluent you know
in all kinds of black slums

2

Charfering-homa
talking-man
policeman
can't interfere with us we're
sanctioned Punch is exempt
out of the Police Act some's
very good men & some
tyrants but generally speaking they're

all werry kind to us
& allows us every
privilege that's a flattery
you know because you'd better
not meddle with them
civility always
gains its esteem

3
A sailor & a
lass half-seas over
we like best of
all he will tip
his mag we always
ensure a few pence
& sometimes a shilling
of them we are
fond of sweeps too
they're a sure brown
if they've got one
& they'll give before
many a gentleman but
what we can't abide
nohow is the shabby
genteel them altray cativa
& no mistake they'll
stand with their mouths
wide open like a
nutcracker & is never
satisfied & is too
grand even to laugh

it's too much trouble
to carry ha'pence
& they've never no
change or else they'd
give us some they've
no money at all
they wants it all
for &c.

4
Once too when I
was scarpering with my
culling in the monkey
I went to mendare
the cativa slums in
a churchyard & sat down
under the tombs to
stitch 'em up a
bit thinking no-one would
varder us there but
Mr.Crookshank took us
off there as we
was a sitting I
know I'm the same
party 'cos Joe seen
the print & draw'd
quite nat'ral with the
slumares a laying about
on all the tombstones
round us in print

5

Punch was taken from
Italy by Porsini lived
like the first nobleman
in the land &
realized an immense deal
of money during his
lifetime I've heard tell
he used to take
very often as much
as 10 pounds a-day &
now it's come down
to little more than
10 pence & he used
to sit down to his
fowls & wine &
the very best of
luxuriousness like the first
nobleman in the world
such as a bottle
of wine he reduced
himself to want &
died in the workhouse
he didn't ought
to have been let
die where he did
but misfortunes will happen
to all every one
in London knowed him
lords dukes squires princes
& wagabones all used

to stop & laugh
his name is writ
in the annuals of
history & handed down
as long as grass
grows & water runs

6

when we are dwelling on orders
we goes along the streets
chirripping rootooerovey
ooey-ooey-ooerovey
that means any more wanted?
That's the pronounciation of the
call in the old Italian style
tooroveyto-roo-to-roo-toroo-torooey
we does when we are
dwelling for orders mostly
at noblemen's houses it
brings the juvenials
to the window & causes
the greatest of attractions to
children of noblemen's families
rich & poor
lords dukes earls
& squires
& gentlefolks

7

Always Mr. Punch when he
performs to nobleman's juvenile parties

he requires a little refreshment
& sperrits before commencing because
the performance will go far
superior but where teetotallers is
he plays very mournful &
they don't have the best
parts cos pump-vater gives
a person no heart to
exhibit his performance where if
any sperrits is given to
him he would be sure to
give the best of satisfaction
I likes where I goes
to perform for the gennelman
to ring the bell &
say to the butler to bring
this here party up whatever
he chooses Punch he likes
the best not particular to
brandy for fear of his
nose of fading & afeerd
of his losing the colour

8
now it's all over
this time boys
go home say
your prayers we says
& steps it such
scenes of life we

see no person would
hardly credit what we
go through we travel
often yeute munjare &
oftentimes we're in fluence
according as luck runs

9
Punch is like
the rest of
the world he
has got bad
morals but very
few of them

XXXVI

I

I don't keep no accounts of what I gets
or what I spends
it would be no use
money comes & it goes
& it often goes a damned sight faster
than it comes so it seems to me
though I ain't in debt
just at this time
I suppose grub costs 1*s.* a day
& beer 6*d.* but
I keeps no accounts
I buy ready-cooked meat
often cold b'iled beef
& eats it at any tap-room I have
meat every day
mostly more than once a day
wegetables I don't care about
only ingans & cabbage
if you can get it smoking hot
with plenty of pepper

the rest of my tin goes
for rent & baccy & togs
& a little drop of gin now & then

2

We couldn't live on what
we get & yet we
can live on a precious
little here a meal for
five farthings a farthing's worth
of coffee a farthing's worth
of sugar & half a
pound of bread three farthings
a slap-up dinner for
two-pence a common one
for a penny oh yes
a regular roarer for two
pence three halfpenny worth of
pudding & a halfpenny worth
of gravy or else we
can have 2½ lb. of taturs
that's a penny & ½ lb
fourpenny bacon that's another
penny what we calls a
first-rate dinner often we're
forced to put up with a
penn'orth of taturs & a
halfpenny herring that's a three-
halfpenny dinner

there's a chap here was
forced to do today with
a ha'p'orth of taturs he's
been out ever since &

perhaps won't come in at
all tonight he'll walk the
streets & starve

3
People that's quality that's
my notion on it
that hasn't neither to
yarn their dinner nor
to cook it but
just open their mouths
& eat it
can't dirty their hands so
at dinner as to
have glasses to wash
'em in arterards but
there's queer ways everywhere

XXXVII

1

I saw Manning & his wife hung
Mrs. Manning was dressed beautiful when she
came up she screeched when Jack Ketch
pulled the bolt away she was harder
than Manning they all said without her
there would have been no murder it
was a punishment to her to come
on the scaffold & see Manning with
the rope about his neck if people
takes it in the right light I
did 4s.6d. at the hanging two handkerchiefs
& a purse with 2s. in it
the best purse I ever had I've
only done three or four I've never
been well dressed if I went near
a lady she would say tush tush
you ragged fellow & would shrink away
but I would rather rob the rich
than the poor they miss it less
but 1s. honest goes further than 5s.
stolen some call that only a saying
but it's true all the money I
got soon went most of it a-gambling
picking pockets is the daringest thing a
boy can do it didn't frighten me
to see Manning & her hanged I
never thought I'd come to the gallows

& I never shall I'm not high-tempered
enough for that the only thing that
frightens me when I'm in prison is
sleeping in a cell by myself you
do in the Old Horse & the
Steel because I think things may appear
you can't imagine how you dreams in
trouble I've often started up in a
fright from a dream I don't know
what might appear I've heard people talk
about ghosts & once in the County
a tin had been left under a
tap that went drip drip drip &
all in the ward were shocking frightened
& weren't we glad when we found
out what it was

2

We might have done very well indeed
out of the Mannings I've been through
Hertfordshire Cambridgeshire & Suffolk along with
George
Frederick Manning & his wife travelled
from 800 to 1,000 miles with 'em
but I could have done much better
if I had stopped in London every
day I was anxiously looking for a
confession from Mrs. Manning all I wanted
was for her to clear her conscience
afore she left this here whale of

tears & when I read in the
papers that her last words on the
brink of eternity was I've nothing to
say to you Mr. Rowe but to
thank you for your kindness I guv
her up entirely had completely done with
her the public looks to us for
the last words of all monsters in
human form & as for Mrs. Manning's
they were not worth the printing

3

the last dying speeches & executions are
all printed the day before they're always
done on Sunday if the murderers are
to be hung on Monday I've been
& got them myself on the Sunday
night over & over again the flying
stationers goes with the papers in their
pockets & stand under the drop &
as soon as ever it falls &
long before the breath is out of
the body they begin bawling out here
is printed & published the last dying
speech & confession of George Frederick Manning
who was executed this morning at Horsemonger
Lane Gaol for the murder of Mr.
Patrick O'Connor at Minver-place Bermondsey &
they dress it up just as they
think will tell best tell the biggest

lies they think of say the man
made a full confession when maybe he
never said a word & there is
not a syllable in the paper here
you have also an exact likeness they
say of the murderer taken at the bar
of the Old Bailey when all the
time it is an old wood-cut
that's been used for every criminal
for the last forty years

XXXVIII

1
A man that's never been to
school an hour can go &
patter a dying speech or battle
between two ladies of fortune they're
what we call running-patters you're
obliged to keep moving on with
them they require no scholarship at
all you want is to stick
a picture on your hat to
attract attention & to make all
the noise you can it's all
the same when they does an
Assassination of Louis Philippe or a
Diabolical Attempt on the Life of
the Queen a good stout pair
of lungs & plenty of impudence
is all that is required but
to patter Bounce the workhouse beadle
& the examination of the paupers
before the Poor-law Commissioners takes
a good head-piece & great
gift of the gab let me
tell you

2
The West End is very good
the early part of the week

for anything that's genteel such as
the Rich Man & his Wife
quarrelling because they have no family
our customers there are principally footmen
grooms & maid-servants the East
End of the town is best
on Friday & Saturday evenings I
very often go to Limehouse on
Friday evening most part of the
dock-men are paid then & anything
comic goes off well among them

3
I did very well with the
Burning of the House of Commons
I happened by accident to put
my pipe into my pocket amongst
some of my papers & burnt
them I told the people my
burnt papers were parliamentary documents rescued
from the flames & that as
I dare not sell them I
would let them have a straw
for a penny & give them
one of the papers by this
trick I got rid of my
stock twice as fast & got
double the price that I should
have done the papers had nothing
at all to do with the

House of Commons some was Death
& the Lady & Death &
the Gentleman & others were the
Political Catechism & 365 lies Scotch English
& Irish & each lie as
big round as St. Paul's

XXXIX

1

I can't work much more than
four hours a-day on the pipes
for the blowing knocks me up
& leaves me very weak

I've never had a day's health
ever since I left the regiment I have
pains in my back & stitches in the side

my girl can't dance without my playing
when I give over she must give over too

I never ax anybody for money
anybody that don't like to give
we never ax them

2

When I'm marching through
the streets & playing
on the pipes I
always carry my head
high up in the
air & throw my
legs out well the
boys will follow for
miles some of them
the children very often

lose theirselves from following
me such a way

3
I've never been ill-treated by
boys but a drunken man often
on a Saturday night gives me a push
or a knock they'll begin dancing
around me a mob will collect
& sets the police onto me I always
play a slow tune when drunken men they
can't dance they'll ask for a
quick tune I won't play one they'll
hit me or push me about the police
never interfere unless a mob collects
& then they are obliged
by their regulations
to interfere

4
I can live in Scotland much cheaper than here

I can give the children
a good breakfast of oatmeal-porridge
every morning
in seven weeks
will make them as fat as
seven years of tea & coffee here

I'm thinking of sending my family down to Scotland
& sending them money I earn in London

they'll have to walk to Hull
& then take the boat they can
get to Aberdeen from there

we shall have to work the money on the road

XL

1

Here I must have money
for I won't go home 'til morning
'til morning 'til morning
I won't go home 'til morning
'til daylight does appear
& so I may as well
sell my old fiddle myself as
take it to a rogue of a broker try it
anybody it's a fine old tone equal
to any Cremonar it cost me
two guineas & another fiddle
& a good'un too in exchange but
I may as well be my own broker
for I must have money any how
& I'll sell it for 10s

2

There'll always be something done in it
as long as you can find young men
that's conceited about their musical talents
fond of taking their medicine if I've
gone into a public-house room
where I've seen a young gent that's bought a
duffing fiddle of me it
don't happen once in twenty times that he
complains & blows up about it
& only then perhaps

if he happens to be drunkish when
people don't much mind what's said
& so it does me no harm people's
too proud to confess they're ever done
at any time or in anything why
such gents has pretended
when I've sold 'em a duffer
& seen them afterwards that
they've done *me*

3

I sat down by the last bit of coal in the place
& sat a long time thinking
& didn't know what to do there was nothing
to hinder me going out in the morning
& working the streets with a mate
as I'd done before but there was
little James sleeping there in his bed
he was very delicate then to drag him about
& let him sleep in lodging-houses
would have killed him I knew but
I couldn't think of parting with my violin
I felt I should never again
have such another I felt
to part with it was parting with my last prop
for what was I to do?
I sat a long time thinking
my instrument on my knees
'til I'm sure I don't know how to describe it I felt
as if I was drunk though I hadn't even tasted beer

so I went out boldly just as if I *was* drunk
& with a deal of trouble
persuaded a landlord I knew to lend me £1
on my instrument & keep it by him
for three months 'til I could redeem it I
have it now

XLI

Ay it's only Dutch now
as is second-handed in the streets
but it'll soon be Americans

the swags is some of them
hung up with Slick's they're
hung up with 'em sir
& no relation whatsomever'll
give a printed character of 'em

& so they must come to the streets
& jolly cheap they'll be

XLII

1

Its very hard work
for the horses in busses
starting after stopping
is the hardest work it's
such a terrible strain I've felt
for the poor things
on a wet night with a bus
full of big people

2

it's a pity anybody uses
a bearing rein there's
not many uses it now it
bears up a horse's head
& he can only go on pulling
pulling up a hill one way
if a man had to carry a weight
up a hill on his back
how would he like to
have his head tied back?

3

I must keep
exact time at
every place a
time-keeper's stationed
not a minute's excused there's
a fine for the least delay

I can't say that it's often
levied but still
we are liable to it

if I've been blocked I must
make up for the block
by galloping &
if I'm seen to gallop I'm
called over the coals

I must drive as quick
with a thunder-rain pelting in my face
& the roads in a muddle
& the horses starting at
every flash just as
quick as if it was
a fine hard road
& fine weather

4
It's not easy to drive a 'bus
but I can drive & must drive
to an inch yes sir
to half an inch I know
if I can get my horses' heads
through a space I can
get my splinter-bar through I
drive by my pole making
it my centre if I keep it
fair in the centre a carriage
must follow unless it's

slippery weather & then
there's no calculating

5

A 'bus changes horses
four or five times a-day
according to the distance

every horse in our stables
has one day's rest in
every four but
it's no rest for the driver

6

I've asked for a day's holiday
& been refused I was
told I might take
a week's holiday if I liked or
as long as I lived

7

In winter I never see
my three children only
as they're in bed & I
never hear their voices
if they don't wake up early

if they cry at night it
don't disturb me I sleep so
heavy after fifteen hours' work
out in the air

8
I can't be said to
have any home just a
bed to sleep in I'm
never ten minutes awake in
the house where I lodge

XLIII

1

many a lady's pony harness
goes next to a tradesman
& next to a costermonger's donkey

& if it's been good leather to begin with
as it will if it was made for a lady
why the traces'll stand clouting

& patching & piecing & mending
for a long time & they'll
do to cobble old boots last of all

for old leather'll wear
just in treading
when it might snap at a pull

2

I suppose it's this way
the garret-master buys lasts
to do the slop-snobbing cheap
mostly women's lasts
& he dies or is done up &
goes to the great house
& his lasts find their way
back to the streets you
notice sir the first time you're
in Rosemary-lane how little

a great many of the lasts have
been used & that
shows what a terrible
necessity there was
to part with them
in some there's hardly any
peg-marks at all

3
There's so much to look at you
understand sir if you wants a decent set
& don't grudge a shilling or two
& I never grudges them myself
when I has 'em
so it takes a little time you
must see the buckles has good tongues
& it's a sort of joke in the trade
a bad tongue's a damned bad thing
& that the pannel of the pad
ain't as hard as a board
flocks is the best stuffing sir
& that the bit if it's rusty
can be polished up for a
animal no more likes a rusty bit in his mouth
than we likes a musty bit of bread in our'n

O a man as treats his ass
as a ass
ought to be treated
& it's just the same if he has a pony

can't be too perticler
if I had my way I'd 'act a law
making people perticler
about 'osses' & asses' shoes
if your boot pinches you sir
you can sing out to your bootmaker
but a ass can't blow up a farrier

XLIV

I

if a pouncey's girl
or a girl he knows
seems in luck if she
picks up a gentleman
partickler if he's drunk
the pouncey I've
seen it many a time
jumps out of the ranks he
keeps a look-out for the spoil
& he drives to her it's
the pounceys too that mostly
go gagging where the girls walk
it's such a set we have to deal with
only yesterday an
out-&-out pouncey called me
such names about nothing it's
shocking for any female that
may be passing aye
& of a busy night in the Market
when it's an opera-night
& a play-night the gentlemen's
coachmen's as bad
for bad language &
some gentlemen's very
clever at that sort of language too

2

Swells now think as
much of one shilling
as they did of twenty then
but there's some swells left still

one young swell brings
four quarts of gin
out of a publichouse in a pail
& the cabmen must drink it
out of pint pots he's
quite master of bad language if
they don't drink fairly

another swell gets a gallon of gin
always from Carter's
& cabmen must drink it
out of quart pots no other way

it makes some of them mad drunk
& makes them drive like mad
for they might be half drunk to begin with

3

There's no racketier place in the
world than the Market
houses open all night
& people going there after
Vauxhall & them places
after a masquerade at Vauxhall I've seen

cabmen drinking with lords & gentlemen but
such lords get fewer every day
& cockney tars that was
handy with their fists wanting to
fight Highlanders that wasn't
& the girls in all sorts of dresses
here & there &
everywhere among them the
paint off & their dresses torn

XLV

I've often laughed & said
I could say what
perhaps nobody or almost
nobody in England can say now

that I'd been driven
by a king he
grew to be a king afterwards
George the fourth

one night you see sir
I was called off the stand
& told to take up
at the British Coffee-house

in Cockspur Street
when I pulled up at the door
the waiter ran out
said you jump down

& get inside
the Prince is a-going to
drive hisself I didn't much
like the notion on it

but I didn't exactly know
what to do & was getting
off my seat to see
if the waiter had put anything inside

for he let down the glass
& just as I was getting down
& had my foot on the wheel
out came the Prince of Wales

& four or five
rattlebrained fellows
like himself I had
hardly time to see them

the Prince gripped me
by the ankle
& the waistband of my breeches
& lifted me off the wheel

& flung me right into the coach
through the window
& it was opened
as it happened luckily

he didn't seem so
very drunk either
& drove very well
for a prince

but he didn't take the
corners or the crossings
careful enough
for a regular jarvey

it was a gaming-house
he went to that night
but I have driven him
to other sorts of

houses in that there
neighbourhood he hadn't
no pride to such as me
hadn't the Prince of Wales

XLVI

1

I know the Duke
very well he's very
kind to his clan
he's Campbell clan &
so am I he
never spoke to me
but he told the
servants to give me
dinner every time I
came that way the
servants told me the
Duke had promised me
my dinner every time
I came when I
touch my bonnet he
always nods to me
he never gave me
only a shilling once
but always my dinner
that's better for me

2

Gentlemen are too good judges of horse-flesh
to put up with poor cattle even though
they may wear slop coats themselves
& rig their servants out in slop liveries
nothing shows a gentleman more
than his horse

3
I know nothing
about what income tax
means but it's some roguery
as is
put on the poor

4
At last I took a notion
of puttin so much every Sathurday night
in the savin bank & faith sir
that was the lucky notion for me
though Peggy wouldn't hear of it
at all at all she swore the bank
'ud be broke & said she could
keep the goold safer in her own stockin
that thim gintlemin in banks were
all a set of blickards & only
desaved the poor people
into givin them their money
to keep it thimselves

5
On a Sunday anybody
would think him the
first nobleman or squire
in the land to
see him dressed in
his white hat with
black crape round it
his drab paletot &

mother-o'-pearl buttons
black kid gloves fingers
too long for him

XLVII

1

one day I went for a load & a half of lime
& where you fetches a load & a half of lime
they always gives you fourpence so
as I was having a pint of beer out of it
my master come by & saw me drinking
& give me the sack
then he wanted me to ax his pardon
& I might stop
but I told him
I wouldn't beg no one's pardon
for drinking a pint of beer as was give me
so I left there

2

I got some work with a rubbish carter
a regular scurf I made only about 8s. a week under him
for he didn't want me this half day or that whole day
& if I said anything he told me
I might go & be damned
he could get plenty such
& I knew he could

3

hadn't a stroke of work for a fortnight
& very little for two months
& if my wife hadn't had middling work with a laundress
we might have starved

or I might have made a hole in the Thames
it's no good
living to be miserable & feel
you can't help yourself any how

4
I look on it that
washing labour is part
of the wife's keep or
what she gives
in return for it as
she'd have to be kept
if she didn't do it
why there shouldn't be no
mention of it if she was
working for others it would be
quite different but washing
is a family matter that's
my way of looking at it

5
& I had again to apply for relief
& got an order for the stone-yard
to go & break stones ten bushels for 15*d*
my hands got all blistered & bloody
& I've gone home &
cried with pain & wretchedness at first
it was on to three days
before I could break ten bushels I felt
shivered to bits all over

my arms & shoulders & my head
was splitting & got to
do it in two days
& then in one
& it grew easier

6
I've worked eleven years in the dock
as an extra & it don't give
more than 5s. in the week why
we're very often three or four weeks
& earn nothing in the winter time
we goes about jobbing doing things
down at Billingsgate we gets a twopenny
& a three-halfpenny job very often
if we don't get that we have
to go without anything for lodging &
walk & starve I'll have to do
that tonight sir I'll have to walk
the streets all night

7
O I do middling I
live by one thing
or other &
when I die
there'll just be
enough to
bury the old man

XLVIII

1

I was a mason's labourer
Smith's labourer plasterer's
labourer bricklayer's labourer a
labouring man I
could not get employment

I was for six months without
any employment

2

The poor mechanic will
sit in the casual wards
like a lost man
scared it's shocking to
think a decent mechanic's houseless

when he's beat out he's
like a bird out of a cage he
doesn't know where to go
or how to get a bit

3

was once out of work a mistake
a good many weeks
five or six or more

I larned then what short grub meant
I got a drop of beer

& a crust sometimes
with men as I knowed
or I might have dropped in the street

the days seemed wery long
but I went about &
called at dust-yards
till I didn't like
to go too often
& I met men I know'd at tap-rooms

4
I once fell down in the Cut
from hunger & I was
lifted into Watchorn's he said
give the poor fellow a little drop of brandy
& after that a biscuit the
best things he can have he
saved my life sir the people at the bar
they see'd it was no humbug
gathered sevenpence ha'penny for me
a penny a-piece & a poor woman
as I was going away
slipt a couple of trotters into my hand

5
I've been in most trades
besides
been a pot-boy both
boy & man

& I could get a pot-boy's place again
but I'm not so strong as I were
& it's slavish work
in the place I could get

& a man that's not so
young as he was once
is chaffed so by the young lads
& fellows in the tap-room
& the skittle-ground

6
I thought I'd be
by this time
toes up in
Stepney churchyard
grinning at the lid
of an old coffin

XLIX

If it had been a fat ox
that had to be accommodated
before he was roasted
for an alderman they'd have
found some way to do it but
it don't matter for poor men
though why we shouldn't be
suited with a market as well as
richer people is not the ticket
that's the fact

L

1

The last sewer I was working at
was that sewer at Blackfriars-bridge that
played the deuce with me that did

we pulled up an old sewer had
been down upwards of 100 years &
under this a burying-ground we dug
up I should think one day about
seven skulls & as to leg-bones
oh a tremendous lot of leg-bones
to be sure I don't think men
has got such leg-bones now the
stench was dreadful we knocked off day-
work & was put on to night-
work to hide it after that bout
I was ill at home for a week

2

we nails our lanterns up
to the crown of the
sewer when the slide is
lifted up the rush is
very great & takes all
before it roars away like
a wild beast we're obligated
to put our heads fast
up against the crown &

bear on our shovels so
not to be carried away
& taken bang into the
Thames there's nothing for us
to lay hold on if
taken off our legs there's
a heavy fall about three
feet just before you comes
to the mouth if we
was to get there the
water is so rapid nothing
could save us

3
Great black
rats as
would frighten
a lady into
asterisks to
see
of a sudden

LI

1

but this is the way
if I am buying second-hand things
at a broker's or in Petticoat Lane
or anywhere & there's a pistol seems cheap
I'll buy it as readily as
anything I know & I'll soon sell it
at a public-house or
I'll get it raffled for
second-hand pistols sell better than new
by such as me if there's a
little silver-plate let into the wood
& a crest or initials engraved on it
I've got it done sometimes there's
a better chance of sale

2

I gave only 7s. 6d. for this pistol
& refused 10s. 6d.
I'll get a better price
I bought it to take to Ascot races
& have it with me now
it's not loaded for I'm going to Moulsey Hurst
where Hampton races are held you're
not safe if you travel after a
great muster at a race by yourself
without a pistol many a poor fellow like me
has been robbed & the public hear
nothing about it or
say it's all gammon

LII

1

I vos at von time a coster
riglarly brought up to the business

the times vas good then but lor
ve used to lush at sich a rate

about ten year ago I ses
to meself I say Bill
I'm blowed if this here
game'll do any longer

I had a good moke
& a tidyish box ov a cart
so vot does I do but goes
& sees von o' my old pals
that gits into the coal-line somehow

he & I goes to the
Bell & Siven Mackerels
in the Mile End Road
& then he tells me all he knowed
& takes me along vith hisself
& from that time I sticks to the coals

2

I niver cared much about the lush myself
& ven I got avay from the old uns
I didn't mind it no how

but Jack my pal vos a awful lushy cove
he couldn't do no good
at nothink votsomever

he died they say of *lirium trumans*
vich I takes to be too much of
Trueman & Hanbury's heavy

LIII

1

I've had men dressed like
gentlemen no doubt they was
respectable when they was sober
bring two or three books
or a nice cigar case
or anythink that don't show
in their pockets & say
drunk as blazes give me
what you can for this
I want it sold for
a particular purpose more drink
I should say & I've known
the same men come back
in less than a week
& buy what they'd sold
& be glad if I
had it by me still

2

poor people run to such
as me I've known them
come with such things as
teapots & old hair mattresses
& flock beds & then
I'm sure they're hard up
reduced for a meal I
don't like buying big things

like mattresses though I do
sometimes some are as keen
as Jews at a bargain
others only anxious to
get rid of the things
& have hold of some bit of
money anyhow yes sir I've
known their hands tremble
to receive the money & mostly
the women's they haven't been used to it

3
Last week a man in black
he didn't seem rich
came into my shop
looked at some old books
& said have you any black lead
he didn't speak plain
& I could hardly catch him I said
no sir I don't sell black lead
but you'll get it at No. 27
but he answered not black lead
black letter speaking very pointed
I said no & I haven't a
notion what he meant

LIV

1

I picked up with a man
Jack Williams had no legs he
was an old sailor got frost
bitten in the Arctic regions I
used to lead him all about
Ratcliffe Highway & sometimes up as
far as Notting Hill with a
big painted board afore him a
picture of the place where he
was froze in I was with
him for fifteen months till one
night I said something when he
was a-bed didn't please him
he got his knife out &
stabbed my leg in two places

here are the marks

2

I can only see hisself sir
He's sure to give me any
coppers he has
in his coat-pocket
& that's a very great thing
to a poor man like me

3
It's no use
such as us
calling at fine houses
to know if they've
any old keys to
sell no we
trades with the poor

4
O yes I'll buy bones
if I have any ha'pence
rather than go without but
I pick them up
or have them
given to me
mostly

LV

1

When I set out on a country round
& I've gone as far as Guildford & Maidstone
& St. Alban's I
lays in as great a stock of
glass & crocks as I can raise money for
or my donkey or pony
can drag without distressing him

I swops my crocks for anythink in the second-hand way
& when I've got through them
I buys outright & so
works my way back to London

I stay at the beer-shops & little inns
some of the landlords looks very shy
if you're a stranger acause
if the police detectives is after anythink
they go as hawkers or barrowmen
or somethink that way

I've very seldom slept in a common lodging-house
I'd rather sleep on my barrow

2

In lodging-houses the air is
very bad enough to stifle you
in bed so many breaths together

there's people there talk backward for
one they say *eno* for two
owt for three *eerht* for four
ruof for five *evif* for six
exis I don't know any higher

LVI

Last year I helped a man one day
& he did so well on fruit
for he got such a early start
& so cheap he
gave me 3*d*. extra
to go to the play with

I didn't go I
has no amusements

I'd rather go to bed at seven every night
than anywhere else

I'm fond of sleep I never
wakes all night I dreams
now & then but I never
remembers a dream

LVII

I've been bird-selling in the streets
larks linnets goldfinches
for six-&-twenty years & more

I liked the birds &
do still I
used to think

at first they was like me
they was prisoners & I
was a cripple

I don't remember living in any place
but London I remember
being at Stroud though

where my father had taken me
& bathed me often in the sea himself
thinking it might do me good

when I was very young
he took me to almost every hospital in London
but it was of no use

I was born a cripple sir
& I shall die one I
couldn't walk at all until I was six

& I was nine or ten
before I could get up & down stairs
& went among other boys

I was in great distress I was
taunted they were
bad to me then

& they are now
grown persons swearing at me
so life was

a burthen to me
as I've read something about
I've sat down & cried

but not often
I like to sit out in the sunshine
& of course a deal of thoughts

goes through my head I think
shall I be able to afford myself plenty of bread
when I get home?

& I think of the next world sometimes
& feel quite sure I shan't be a cripple yes
that's a comfort for this world will

never be any good to me & it's
nothing to me who's king
or who's queen it can

never have anything to do with me
I shall be a poor starving cripple till I end
perhaps in the workhouse I dream

most about starving
when I have to go to sleep hungry
more than once I

dreamed I was starving &
dying of hunger I remember I woke
in a tremble but most dreams is

soon forgot I've never seemed
to myself to be a cripple in my dreams
I can't explain how but

I feel as if my limbs was
all free like so
beautiful

LVIII

1

Nobody can describe the misery I
walked the streets all night
falling asleep as I went along then
roused myself half frozen
limbs aching if I could
find a penny I'd
sit up in a coffee-shop in Covent-garden
till five in the morning to
roam the streets all day long
careless what my fate would be

2

Monday night I was in the streets
all night without a bite no place to
put my head in &
frightened I walked
the streets all that
cold night I feel
the cold of that night
in my limbs still
I thought it never
would be over

The one-legged sweeper at Chancery Lane

AFTERWORD

Mayhew's initial investigations for the *Morning Chronicle* are published in a selection with two important essays by Thompson and Yeo:

Thompson, E.P., & Yeo, E., eds, (1973) *The Unknown Mayhew*, London: Penguin.

Mayhew's complete *Morning Chronicle* writings have subsequently been published:

Mayhew, H. (1980) *The Morning Chronicle Survey of Labour and the Poor: The Metropolitan Districts*, ed. P. Razzell, 6 Vols, London: Caliban Books

There is a modern reprint of the whole of *London Labour and the London Poor*:

Mayhew, H. (1968) *London Labour and the London Poor* [1861-2], 4 volumes, New York: Dover

There are also three useful selections, each providing additional biographical and critical material:

Mayhew, H. (1965) *Selections from London Labour and the London Poor*, edited by John L.Bradley, London: Oxford University Press

Mayhew, H. (1971) *Voices of the Poor: selections from the Morning Chronicle*, ed. Anne Humpherys, London: Cassell

Mayhew, H. (1985) *London Labour and the London Poor*, ed.V.Neuberg, London: Penguin

For a valuable biography and critical study of Henry Mayhew see:

Humpherys, A. (1977) *Travels into the Poor Man's Country. The work of Henry Mayhew*, London: Caliban Books

From the thousands of printed pages of Mayhew's investigations I have selected a few hundred extracts from those passages where he attempted to record the voices of London's working people. Occasional material in italics is adapted from Mayhew's own commentary.

Brief lives, a moment in time — costermongers, coalheavers, sewermen, seamstresses, soldiers, shopkeepers, domestic servants, old-clothes dealers, rag-and-bone men, petty thieves, prostitutes, street people and casual workers of all kinds, old and young, male and female, thousands of unnamed and unremembered people of mid-nineteenth-century London fill Mayhew's pages. Like him, I have tried to listen to their voices and to the experiences they represent. Selecting passages that I reacted to more or less instantly as I was reading, I have cut and rearranged, setting them on the page in ways which are intended to make them both more readable and less easily or quickly read, sometimes feeling that I was getting closer to the actual voices of these people in the streets of London 150 years ago.

William Carlos Williams said that poetry needs to renew itself by tapping into the energies of common speech. There are energies here generated from sources outside of Mayhew and I've tried to register them. I've added nothing I hope but a sensitive ear and some different ways of representing patterns of speech on paper. The influence here not just of Williams but of a tradition of American writing – Reznikoff, Zukofsky, Oppen, Olson, Dorn, Creeley and others – will be obvious. There are two collections which I'd particularly like to mention:

    Charles Reznikoff, *Testimony. The United States 1885-1890. Recitative*,
    New York: New Directions, 1965
    Ed Dorn, *Recollections of Gran Apacheria*, San Francisco: Turtle
    Island, 1974

The street rhubarb and spice-seller

Printed in the United Kingdom
by Lightning Source UK Ltd.
118240UK00001B/130-132